EVERY MOVE
MUST HAVE A
PURPOSE

EVERY MOVE MUST HAVE A PURPOSE

Strategies from Chess for Business and Life

BRUCE PANDOLFINI

HYPERION

NEW YORK

Library of Congress Cataloging-in-Publication Data

Pandolfini, Bruce.

    Every move must have a purpose : strategies from chess for business and life / Bruce Pandolfini.—1st ed.

      p. cm.

    ISBN: 0-7868-6885-6

    1. Strategic planning.   2. Success in business.
3. Success—Psychological aspects.   4. Chess—
Psychological aspects.   1. Title.

HD30.28.P286 2003

650.1—dc21   2003044964

Hyperion books are available at special quantity discounts to use as premiums or for special programs, including corporate training. For details, contact Michael Rentas, Manager, Inventory and Premium Sales, 77 West 66th Street, 11th floor, New York, New York 10023, or call 212-456-0133.

FIRST EDITION

10   9   8   7   6   5   4   3   2   1

To Ben Franklin, the first American to write a chess book
with the business of life in mind

CONTENTS

EVERY MOVE
MUST HAVE A
PURPOSE

INTRODUCTION

The position on the board can be simple or complex. It doesn't matter. One player thinks he's winning. The other knows he is. Could both be right?

Physicist Niels Bohr said it: The opposite of one great truth is another great truth. Chess illustrates that, move by move. A vulnerable king can be used as a weapon. The lowly pawn can beat the lofty queen. It can even become it. You can calculate, but maybe there's a simple rule. You try it, but it doesn't apply. Or it does, and there's an exception. So you're going to lose. But suddenly, there's a brilliant move. Now you're going to win—if you can only avoid a draw.

Almost any claim about chess comes with a disclaimer. Less can be more. Further can be closer. Later can be sooner. Chessplayers will take either side of a good bet. They operate on the basis of the counterintuitive imperative. And they think diagonally.

On the chessboard, a slanted row of same-color squares is a diagonal. In the real game, an all-purpose path is a diagonal shortcut. The right one can be used to reach a strategic point faster than by any other means. Players who seek chessic wormholes think diagonally. They're not restricted by preconceptions. Resourceful, perceptive, flexible, imaginative, and pragmatic—they can make something out of nothing or reduce a great complexity to its bare essentials.

As a teenager, I studied with a former Wall Street broker. Harry had a saying for everything, and he was usually on the money. But if you repeated a phrase he coined, he'd promptly disburse the flip side of his own advice.

His point? There are always at least two sides to

every question. Most of us play by the same principles, whether they apply or not. But what each side rules in, the other can rule out, especially from the other side.

Harry used what he had learned on Wall Street to teach chess. "Don't consider everything," he'd say, "just everything that matters." His aphorisms had the dialectic edge of years spent contending with market vicissitudes. They taught me to handle adversity, to rebound from setbacks, and to redefine my goals.

Naturally, I tried turning Harry's wheeling-and-dealing approach to chess on its head. And that works too. Chess principles make excellent advice in the business world. Seize the initiative. Play with a plan. Look at your opponent's moves. Don't waste material. Seek small advantages. Everyone who wants to succeed at business or chess must follow these precepts. Skill in either sphere can be expressed in similar terms.

This book combines anecdotes and inquiry to explore fifteen vital chess principles. It also includes stories and insights about some of chess history's greatest players. Much here transcends chess and applies directly to life.

Chessplayers make it their business to master both the obvious and the ambiguous. Their rules are as straightforward as they are subtle. But chess is not the mere play of contradictions. It's also a contest, and for real, just like business. Great truths are true for any game. Chess and business. The two worlds might be different if they weren't so alike. Success in either could be hard if it weren't so simple.

Find one truth and you find another.

1.

Play the Board, Not the Player

Chess point: Everything pertinent to the
game can be learned from the position of the
pieces on the board.

Some years ago I was asked to give an exhibition at
a New York City establishment for troubled teen-
agers. Chessplayers call this sort of thing a "simul,"
and it involves playing a number of opponents at the
same time. In this case, I confronted twenty young men
sitting in a row, many of whom had already had serious
bouts with the law. Cynical and self-assured, they could
hold their own in any kind of street fight. Clearly, a
chess game held no terrors.

I glanced quickly over the boards. There was one
at the far end of the room that looked strangely askew.

The player sitting there, behind the white pieces, was glowering at me as if we were facing off before the start of a boxing match. I walked over to take a closer look at the board.

Both sides were set up correctly. Each army occupied its first and second ranks. But this inventive fellow had managed to plant an extra rook on his third row. "You have three rooks," I observed. The young man looked me full in the face. "Are you accusing me of cheating?" he asked, his voice laced with implied threat.

Respect your opponent, I told myself, don't fear him. Still, I found myself recalling a past occasion working chessboards with other tough guys. I'd volunteered to teach chess once a week at a nearby penitentiary in New York State.

A lot of riots broke out back then that never made the news, and I was treated to one while I was teaching my class. The guards carefully closed off a wing in order to secure the prison. I was left trapped in the library with twelve miscreants, among them a murderer or two. All the while, I desperately racked my brain to find some astute comments on the importance of cornering the king and the value of attacking in number. Hoping for a bright idea proved unnecessary, however. None of the nearby fuss fazed my students in the slightest. The group continued to play chess as if nothing else mattered.

That memory in mind, I returned to the setup sporting three white rooks. I glanced again at the angry young man who'd assumed he could only win with a head start. The educator in me decided to let him keep his extra piece. Maybe there was a lesson to be learned. But it didn't come to that, for my challenger suddenly removed his third rook and said, "Let's play."

I knew my opponent was insecure about his abilities, so I didn't expect much. During my first few laps around the room, I'd take a brief look at his board, make a move, and head on. Around move twelve, though, I stopped short. From where I stood, it didn't look that great.

The young man was actually quite adept, and our battle turned out to be my toughest game of the day. I had to work pretty hard before I finally found a winning idea. After a grueling struggle, my opponent had merely a king to my king and pawn. I managed to advance the pawn to its eighth rank.

My young adversary looked up at me. We both knew I could exchange the pawn for a new queen. I paused. Then I asked for a rook. Now the extra rook belonged to me, and this one was indisputable, gained according to the rules of the game. Smiling in recognition, my opponent extended his hand in gracious defeat.

What a force that young man turned out to be. Before we started, he had fixated on the player he had to face. But with his first move, he focused his energies on the game. Not his opponent. Not the psych-out. Not the setting. Just the game.

Conversely, I had begun by dismissing my opponent as a novice. In the end, his resolute play forced me to do what all chessplayers must: concentrate on the contest, not the player. We were both back at the quest for truth, and that, in chess, is always found on the board.

Chess is a totality containing perfect information.

Nothing is hidden from us. We can count pieces and discern an advantage in space. We can target weak squares and focus on the opposing king. We can divide our thinking into convenient steps and assess each one. And when it comes to forming plans and making decisions, we learn to abide by what logic dictates and our analysis supports. In the beginning, middle, and end, all the answers are before us, in the positions of the pieces, in the rules of the game, in the moves we make.

Obviously, players are free to use anything that could provide them with constructive information. Why not? In one international competition, Bobby Fischer was about to launch what he thought was a clever attack when he noticed that his adversary had taken on the posture of Rodin's *The Thinker*. Fischer sensed immediately that he was walking into an ambush. He was tipped off by his opponent's body language.

The other player had indeed set a trap. Then he froze, and that betrayed his ruse. But Fischer still had to find good moves to win. Ultimately, the placement of the pieces—not his opponent's petrified posture—gave him the solution he sought.

Many books have been written advising us how to interpret the subtle deportment of our partners, bosses, or employees. Understanding physical clues can be germane to any environment, and all kinds of elusive factors can assist us in making decisions.

Can any of those signals really substitute for the right moves? Not likely. And what if you misinterpret a sign? What if a player dissembles, or disarms you with misleading behavior? What seems like evidence may be disinformation. In short, your opponent might fool you in any number of ways. The board can't. Chess reality is found in the position of the pieces on sixty-four squares, plain and simple.

Surely we can say the same about the business world. Anything from a blink of an eye to a Freudian slip may provide clues to exploit before taking action. But depending on our assumptions can be dangerous. We might misinterpret what we see. What we assume to be clues may turn out to be red herrings.

Accurate information is necessary for good decision making. Sound judgment requires evidence we can count on. Consider anything, but to succeed in the big game, rely on the actual facts.

- **The board can't lie.**

2.

Don't Ignore
a Good Hunch

Chess point: Moves can be right whether or
not they make sense.

No one should sneeze at a hunch. Grandmasters
certainly don't. Take one of the twentieth century's
greatest players, the Latvian Mikhail Tal (1936–1991).
There walked an artist who blended exacting analysis
with intuitive genius. Tal, who at the enterprising age
of twenty-three stole the world championship from the
Russian Mikhail Botvinnik (1911–1995), played sacrifices so complicated they defied objective investiga-
tion. Even so, the eighth world chess champion trusted
his premonitions for good reason. They usually won.

13

Tal used to tell a story about playing grandmaster Yevgeny Vasiukov (b. 1933) at one of the USSR championships. After about twenty moves, the two players had concocted a light-and-dark labyrinth on the board. Confused, Tal considered making a knight sacrifice. But try as he might, he couldn't quite visualize the outcome.

Chess chaos. It can be almost unbearable. Nonetheless, Tal kept trying to sort out the variations running riot in his brain. Unaccountably, a classic line from the Russian poet Korney Ivanovich Chukovsky suddenly popped into his head. "Oh, what a difficult job it was to drag the hippopotamus out of the marsh."

The game was at stake. Tal tried to focus on it. But he couldn't get the hippo out of his mind or off the board. His imagination had planted the beast on a square of its own. How, Tal wondered, would they drag a hippo out of a marsh anyway? Would they use levers, a rope ladder, a helicopter, or what? After a while the hippo and the knight became a dilemma. Finally, in disgust, Tal thought, "Well, let it drown."

At that instant the hippopotamus disappeared from

both Tal's mind and the board. The chess situation no longer seemed complicated. Yet the moves still couldn't be calculated precisely. So Tal said the heck with them too. With no further ado, he sacrificed the knight along with the hippo.

"There are two types of sacrifices," Tal once wrote. "Correct ones and mine." The next day the newspapers were filled with glowing descriptions of Tal's luminous play. Chess commentators expressed astonishment at the amazing knight sacrifice he had worked out over the board. By his own account, however, Tal hadn't worked out anything. He had simply surrendered to feeling. The Latvian wizard chose to cut the Gordian knot by dumping the hippo. He gave way, apparently, to a sixth sense.

Chess by guesswork? Putting your faith in instinct? We're told that there's no such thing as chance when it comes to chess. But if there's no luck, if nothing is adventitious, how could any player at any level depend on a mere impression for a solution?

Chess requires reasoning—deductive and inductive. Players try to crack the code by doing what the board and pieces say is best. They frame a question, gather data, and deduce the right comeback. In this game, logic is supposedly everything.

It's not, of course, and veteran players know it. Even those who can't seem to live without a good algorithm acknowledge that unconscious assumptions can save us when conscious calculation fails. While chessplayers rely on rational thought, we concede this point: There are Dr. Ruth moments. It feels right, so we do it.

We call that a hunch. But intuitive chess comes from a sophisticated ability to perceive blueprints on the board. This sort of pattern recognition is natural, though unconscious. What we think we're feeling we're actually seeing. We've seen it before, or something like it. Look at anything often enough and the image stays with you, providing subconscious proof for decisions you know are correct but can't quite explain.

Over the long haul, players assimilate arrangements and relate them to consequences. Masters create memory chunks containing tens of thousands of chess positions. They draw from a treasury of past experience to problem-solve in the present. Like Tal, agile players may not be able to say why a move makes sense at the moment they make it. But this doesn't stop them from using it to win.

Intuition is no accident. It's an intellectual skill, troubleshooting by association rather than logic. And it turns out that mental suggestion is particularly effective in complex or chaotic situations that might throw off attempts at systematic scrutiny. When there are too many variables to keep in mind, players sometimes slice through the hooey by recognizing and comparing forms and relationships. When they find the best con-figuration, they have their next move.

Business, chess, it doesn't matter. You're more likely to find the right moves, and make the right choices, if you understand that your instincts are based on what you don't know you already do.

And that's not just a hunch.

- **Some moves explain themselves.**

3.

Play with a Plan

Chess point: It's wise to plan, and the best
plans are manageable and flexible.

How far ahead does a master look before playing a
move? At the great New York tournament in
1924, world champion José Raúl Capablanca (1888–
1942) impishly informed a reporter that he often analyzed fifty moves into the future. Grandmaster Reuben
Fine, on the other hand, remarked that he "seldom
looked more than a move ahead, but that was usually
the best one."

Numbers aside, every chessplayer learns to plan
ahead. Every chessplayer has to. Consider perennial
U.S. champion Frank Marshall (1877–1944), founder

of the Marshall Chess Club in New York City's Greenwich Village. Marshall could gamble now and then. But he was equally prepared to study possible sequences and their variations for hours at a time.

Or years. In 1909, at the seasoned age of thirty-two, Marshall played against Capablanca, then a mere chess upstart some eleven years his junior. Over a period of several weeks, Capablanca beat the elder statesman in a match 8–1. Humiliated by the loss, Marshall diligently trained for some future encounter with the Cuban. He developed a curious gambit that seemed to afford him splendid chances regardless of how Capablanca replied, and he practiced in private to keep his plan a secret.

Seven years went by before Marshall's opportunity came knocking. He unveiled his new setup at the Manhattan Chess Club Masters Tournament in New York, and it took everyone by surprise. But not Capablanca, who refuted Marshall's opening over the board, winning handily with purposeful response. Although Capablanca didn't know the variation, it didn't matter.

Why? Because the Cuban master reverted to principles that would inevitably lead to sound chess. By the fifteenth move, Capablanca had found his own counter-plan. "The trapper trapped," he wrote in his autobiography, *My Chess Career*. Once committed, Marshall had no other choice but to continue his plan of attack, "do or die." Marshall did both.

Practically any plan is better than no plan. One that hasn't fared well in one context may do so in another. Marshall's ideas didn't prevail the first time he tried them in a tournament setting. But that didn't make them bad ideas. For over eight decades, chessplayers have burned the midnight oil studying and improving on the Marshall Gambit. Some of the best players, including former world champion Boris Spassky, have played the opening and developed its variations. I've even won with it myself (but let's not go there).

The truth is, Marshall's original plan wasn't terrible. He simply stuck too hard to it. Chess is change. Action and reaction. Every encounter offers a multitude of intricate and layered relationships to disentangle. A reliable plan should be a diagonal one: memorable in its simplicity, compelling in its logic, versatile in its application. Had Marshall been able to play his designs pliantly, he could have made a good plan a great one.

Flexibility counts. So does size. The two work best when they work together. Small and direct plans assure players their ability to adjust quickly, without losing sight of the big picture. Trying to do a few things over the span of no more than several moves, they hope to link these schematic blocks into a grand strategy leading to checkmate.

Players review constantly during the process, making adjustments as needed. When closer to the target, they seek either a new plan or an extension of the current one to carry them toward final victory. As Seneca the Roman once said, if a sailor doesn't know which harbor he's making for, no wind is the right one.

Clearly, rigid preconceptions can lock us in, preventing us from finding alternate routes. Competition may require changing direction at a move's notice. We shouldn't stay with a plan doggedly, without regard to the actual game. We must be supple-minded, for neither the position nor the opponent is likely to calcify.

Fortunately, we have leeway. We can opt for a plan

using Capablanca's intuitive style. Or we can emulate Marshall's hard-work approach. Whatever our method, we should keep our thinking straightforward, definite, and manageable. We should aim for shorter plans, with results easier to predict and control.

Play without a plan, and many things could happen. Most of them are bad. We can't just move pieces and hope for the best, not if we want to win. We can't just buy, not if it's time to sell. Chess and business—they're brain games, where we must see what might happen so we can make it happen our way.

Of course you must plan. Simply make your plans small and adaptable. Then you can find your way home however the wind is blowing.

- **You don't need to plan if you can afford to fail.**

4.

Look at Your Opponent's Moves

Chess point: Nothing should be played without first considering what the opponent has just done.

Back in America's dark ages, just about the time one kid from Brooklyn was about to change the chess world, a different kid from Brooklyn was trying to change his. I remember absolutely. My teacher, Harry, was struggling with one of his students, a Fischer wanna-be. I was there.

I've never forgotten that lesson. Teacher and student sat at a chess table, studying a convoluted position. Finally, Harry asked the teenager what he was thinking. After a minute the student responded, not in words, but by actually playing his next move. Harry reclined in his chair and took a firm look at his adolescent charge. "With what idea?" he asked. Almost immediately the young man reached for a piece, thinking to vindicate himself by moving again.

Once more he heard the question: "With what idea?" The flustered student looked up from the board. Harry cocked an eyebrow. Every player, he said, has to begin by trying to understand his opponent's train of thought. Then he can think through his own.

You also have to be able to explain all this reasoning, Harry added, even if merely to yourself. If you can't detail your decisions during practice sessions, which are devoid of tension and pressure, it might mean you're missing the thread in serious games, when so much more is at stake.

Harry took a moment to let his advice sink in. Then he sighed heavily, leaned forward, and asked his student once again: "With what idea?" Finally, I figured it out. You shouldn't do, without knowing what has to be done. Before you can justify your own moves, you had better analyze your opponent's.

Chessplayers have to scout the rationale behind the

other player's previous move and whether it puts them in peril. Then they can decide if, how, when, and where they should counter. Surely they're thinking all along. But as soon as their opponent's hand leaves the board, all questions become one: What does that move do? Or simply, what is the threat?

If we're facing some danger, we should try to neutralize it, preferably while issuing a threat of our own. If we're not being threatened, we can press on with our own program. Still, and this is central, we shouldn't formulate our plans without evaluating what may just have happened to affect them.

In the ideal state of affairs, moves should always do at least two things in concert: foil our opponent's aims while fostering ours. We can't do either properly if we do only one, and both can be accomplished by first assessing what the other player has done.

In spite of this chess truth, one of the most common mistakes players make is to try an idea independent of the circumstances, from a narrow point of view. Of course it's daunting to look from other or wider perspectives. There are so many changing relationships to monitor. No wonder novices concentrate mainly on their own forces.

Science provides proof. Recent studies have documented a commonsense observation anyone can make by watching a player's eyes. Beginners are generally restricted to scanning their side of the board. Practiced players typically inspect both sides. They gravitate toward the complex interaction between White and Black.

As Frank Sinatra tunefully intoned, it's nice to do things our way. But it makes no sense to ponder giving checkmate if we ignore our opponent's moves and get checkmated first. Chess doesn't allow for last licks, as in so many punchball games back in my old Brooklyn neighborhood. There are consequences to everything, especially paying no attention to what our opponents intend. If you're checkmated, the game is over, and that's that.

It's hard to decide what to attend to. It's harder if you don't attend at all. How do you remedy what you haven't yet diagnosed? After every one of your opponent's moves, the dynamics of chess require that you think through everything relevant, when anything might be.

We return to Harry's point. No one who cares about making a penny, or a fortune, should disregard it. In business or chess, it's not enough to know when to leap. You have to know the reason. So consider your opponent's move. Then decide on yours. Play it, but not if you can't defend your course of action. Nothing should be done unless you can see why. Nothing can be seen if you haven't looked.

- **To see what they see, sit where they sit.**

5.

Don't Waste Material

Chess point: Material should be treated
with respect, according to its existing and
potential value.

A rather dapper gentleman was strolling along the
deck of a cruise ship when he passed a man sitting
before a chessboard, intently analyzing a byzantine position. Emanuel Lasker (1868–1941), the second world
chess champion and a true cosmopolitan, proposed
playing a casual game.

The player looked up from the board, clearly un-
willing to be bothered with a neophyte chancing by.
"How well do you play?" he asked. The mischievous
Lasker admitted he knew a little something about the
game. After some hemming and hawing, his reluctant

opposition allowed him to take a seat. With one condition. "I'll play," the man said, "but only if I can do so without my queen, just to make it interesting for me."

The poor chap had no idea that the best player in the world was sitting across the board, otherwise he'd have realized the absurdity of playing without a queen against someone who could beat him with a chessic flyswatter. Lasker playfully accepted the terms. And though he was ahead by a queen, the world champion deftly managed to lose several games so that he appeared to be what he most definitely wasn't: a meddling patzer.

"You know," Lasker said thoughtfully as he reset the board, "I think it's helpful not to have a queen. Suppose we play again. How about *I* give you the queen odds so I can have the clear space next to my king?" His opponent burst out laughing. The grandmaster persisted. Finally, he convinced the reluctant fellow to start playing with an extra queen. Imagine the guy's confusion when Lasker won several games in a row, citing his singular extra-space thesis as the reason for the success of both players.

Lasker's little fiction was, to be sure, thoroughly ridiculous. Theory reminds us to prefer the tangible to the intangible. No facet tends to be more important than material. Space, time, pawn structure, king safety, and other features of the game play a role in achieving the overall advantage. But no one component is more substantial than material force. We can see it, touch it, and count it.

We can count on it too, for the player with the more powerful arsenal customarily rules. And wins. That's why players sometimes appear insatiable. They want more pieces, and greater ones at that.

Chess pieces are valued according to the number of squares they can attack and defend in unison, the way they move, and their ability to help deliver checkmate. One reason knights and bishops are called "minor" pieces is because neither can checkmate when it stands together with its own king against a solitary opposing king. Rooks and queens are "major" pieces. They certainly can give checkmate, so long as the king is around to help.

While piece values are approximate, they're accepted as reliable. Pawns, generally the weakest unit, are used as the measure of all things in chess. Knights and bishops are worth about three pawns each. A rook is valued at five pawns, and a queen comes in at nine. Not surprisingly, the pawn itself is equal to a mere pawn, even by today's standards and rate of inflation.

Knowing the value of each piece helps us ascertain who gets the better of exchanges. We usually want to get back at least as much as we give up. For a knight, we'd like to get back at least a bishop, or three pawns, or another knight. It's still better to gain a rook for the knight, putting us ahead by two pawns on the deal. Then there's the queen, the most powerful piece (9), though two rooks together ($5 + 5 = 10$) are slightly more valuable.

Material matters. Avoiding material loss while amassing material gain is a typical way players succeed. But chess is also a game that can shift its emphasis in a move's time, an endeavor that relies on the constant reevaluation of particulars. Material value is relative—to the stage of the game, the element of time, and the positional interaction of friendly and enemy forces.

Nowhere is this more obvious than in the life of the humble pawn. Pawns are the every-person of chess pieces, and their moves are permanent. With a rook or bishop, for example, it may be possible to regain one's traction from a misstep. Circumstances permitting, both pieces can be moved back to where they were or somewhere else. Not so with pawns. It's against the rules for pawns to move backward. Once we've made a pawn move, we're stuck with the consequences.

It's natural to think of pawns as being less important. They seem less because they can do less, at least at the start. But their lack of immediate value can render them stalwart in defense, especially as shelter for the king. Lose your king's pawn cover and you're likely to lose far more than a few points in material. You're apt to drop your royal monarch, and thus the game.

That holds mostly for the opening and middle phases of play. Reach an endgame, however, and the little pawn suddenly possesses amazing prospects. If a pawn can get to the other side of the board, it can be promoted to a piece of any kind, except the king. Almost always a promoted pawn is turned into a queen.

Now what's the pawn's real material value? Exceptional. With an extra queen, checkmate is seldom far off. Yet even here, material must be considered in light of the actual. In place and time a player may prefer to have a mere knight, which can do what a high-priced queen can't—jump over barriers to get to the enemy king.

Diagonal thinking requires, above all, a flexible attitude toward every possible factor, including material. Putting a value on each piece helps players analyze the state of their game, decide on the efficacy of trades and sacrifices, or size up an attack. All the same, contenders must understand that any numeric value can rise or fall as conditions fluctuate.

Raw power is basic. Knowing what resources you command and assessing their quality is vital. In business, as in chess, material resources must be analyzed and reappraised at the opening and closing of each business day, and sometimes even during lunch. As

Heraclitus understood long before there were pawns in either chess or big business, flux is inevitable. The value of anything may change. Just the same, resources matter—sometimes how we use them, and sometimes how we don't.

- **You can't save the pieces you've already lost.**

6.

Seize the Initiative

Chess point: To get ahead, it's better to
attack first.

The Ukrainian/German player Efim Bogolubov
(1889–1952) was a superb attacker who eventually
played two world-championship matches with the great
Alexander Alekhine (1892–1946). Bogolubov lost both.
Nevertheless, his flabber was not ghasted. By his own
account, Mr. B couldn't lose, even when he did.

Once asked about how he'd become such a mag-
nificent player, he replied: "When I have the white
pieces I win because I have White. When I have the
black pieces I win because I'm Bogolubov." Curiously,
the same quote is attributed to the Russian Mikhail

Chigorin (1850–1908), but Bogolubov's way of saying it must have been louder. To this day, his admirers may be overheard in nearby rooms.

As Bogolubov so nicely pointed out, White and Black generally share a delusion from the outset. Both act as if they should win the same game. In theory, making the opening move guarantees White a head start. With this slight oomph, White can begin determining the course of play.

Part of the beauty of chess can be found in its apparent contradictions. White does go first. But Black gets to go second! Going first allows you to tender the initial attack. Going second enables you to exploit the mistake your opponent has just made.

Moving first certainly confers a slender advantage, though not a decisive one. Regardless of how White attacks, Black should have ways to keep the position dynamically balanced. Theoretically, if both sides play the best moves possible—White the soundest attacks, Black the perfect counters—every game should end in a draw. Hence, despite White's minimal first-move edge, players are contesting what should remain essentially an equal situation.

Yet few of us play games for the pleasure of drawing. Chessplayers generally sit down intending to vanquish their foes. No matter who moves, the aim is to ignite the process by taking the initiative.

Newcomers learn fairly early that the goal of this universal game is checkmate. But no one can checkmate on the first move. It takes Black at least two moves to do that, after White has blundered just the right way. Funny thing is, it takes White three moves to play an analogous checkmate, which implies that winning quickly depends less on your perfection than on your opponent's imperfection.

The game's length notwithstanding, there's no checkmate without control, and there's no control without seizing the initiative. Possess the initiative and you reap the opportunity to pursue your own plans. The one who has that freedom is most likely to say the magic word that ends the game.

When players usurp the initiative, they take the

reins. Their rivals have to respond to *their* moves, *their* tactics, and *their* strategy. It's a fact of the chessing life: Attackers dictate terms, defenders are compelled to honor them.

Having the initiative grants the attacker more and better options, ranging from slight to serious. He can have more time, more space, or more choice. As a result, the assailant can afford to make a few mistakes that the defender can't.

Why can it be tougher for defenders to survive erroneous play? Because players on the offensive are looking for their opponents to make certain types of moves, those that react to the threats the attacker has planned. So they are particularly in sync to spot moves that don't relate. If the defender misses the point, the attacker is ready to pounce.

When they're trying to protect themselves, however, players simply aren't as prepared to identify and capitalize on their adversary's errors. Their powers are constricted by having to wait and wonder what their antagonists have in store. Generally, their minds are set on figuring ways out of potential predicaments, rather than plaguing their opponents with problems of their own.

Psychology is part of the game too. Attackers typically feel stronger and more confident. When you're on a roll, you don't suppose you can be stopped so easily. And you can't, either, because your mental momentum keeps you going. But when you are on the defensive, fear can keep you gun-shy.

When defenders go amiss, they're apt to suffer immediately. They know they've failed to do what they should have done—prevent their own game from being harmed. When you're already fending off an onslaught, your every gaffe seems worse, to say nothing of the humiliation suffered from a gross oversight. Aggressors are simply more poised, actually and emotionally, to deal with their own missteps.

Whether we're conducting White or Black, whether we go first or second, we have to fight for the initiative in order to acquire practical superiority. If no one has the initiative, we try to get it. When we have the initiative, we try to maintain it. If our opponents have the initiative, we try to snatch it. It's always about the initiative, which is always about control.

Upping the ante in the business world offers more than a hypothetical advantage. It bestows a pragmatic one as well. Entrepreneurial spirit relies on the willingness to attain, keep, and build the initiative. And it's not really that hard to do, to gain command. It's just a matter of tapping the active player inside you—right from the start.

- **When responding, make sure you go first.**

7.

Play for the Center

Chess point: Pieces can do more from the middle.

In my younger days, when I worked as the majordomo at the Manhattan Chess Club, I sometimes sat in on a "happening lesson" to watch other teachers and their students go from chess theory to practice and back again. One day I was cleaning ashtrays, one of my obligatory duties, when I passed by a tired and frustrated teacher. It was almost suppertime, and he and his student had been there for hours. Maybe it had just been a day plagued with students who forgot that the bishop can move backward and that the pawn can't. Who knows? I'd been busy with a lot of ashtrays.

I took a closer look. The teacher was trying to explain a fundamental chess principle: to play for the center. But his student kept moving his pieces away from the middle, especially his knights. Finally, the perturbed teacher plonked a knight back from the rim and asked: "Should you move your knight to the edge, which is bad, or toward the center, which is good?" The student thought for a bit. Then he shrugged, replying: "I don't want to move my knight. I want to move my pawn." Accordingly, he proceeded to push one of his foot soldiers on the right side, far removed from the center.

The teacher tried more irony. "Okay," he said. "If that's the way you want it, I'll just munch on your free pawn." He took hold of his queen and used it to capture a pawn on an outer row. This is called "pawn-grabbing," and it's a cardinal chess sin that's lost many a game, particularly because it tends to remove the game's most powerful piece from circulation. Until the queen can be maneuvered back into position, which usually means bringing it back toward the center, Her Majesty might as well be nowhere.

Once again it was the student's turn. Embarrassed, the poor kid shakily transported his rook all the way across the board to the last horizontal row of squares. "I *think* that's checkmate," he said uncertainly. And to his teacher's bewilderment, it was. While the teacher had temporarily focused his attention on the chessboard's perimeter, the student had won by going through—and past!—the very center of play.

Was the teacher wrong? In this case, yes. He momentarily forgot his own advice about the center, and his own exasperation undid him. He removed his queen from the main theater. He took a "free" pawn standing in the wings. He exposed his king. He lost the game.

The center refers primarily to the four squares in the middle of the board and secondarily to the twelve squares around the inner four. We can guard the center so that it's safe to put our pieces there. We can occupy the center and surrounding territory in order to have greater mobility. We can influence the center by driving away or weakening enemy pieces with central radiance. We can reinforce all of our aims by stopping our op-

ponent from achieving the same central goals we have.
And we can facilitate and expedite by getting there
firstest with the mostest, or by harassing our opponents
with so many threats that they never find any doings of
their own. By using the initiative to command the center, we can direct the flow of the game.

So in the opening phase of chess play, we move our
pieces to central locations. We try to maintain jurisdic-
tion there in the building phase. And we try to use the
center as a base of operations to close out the contest.
At all stages we aim to assert ourselves in the middle,
and we always look there to get our bearings. Ceding
the center practically admits to giving up the fight.

It's natural for newcomers to avoid the center. For
them, placing pieces in the middle is tantamount to
inviting enemy forces to attack. But you have to expect
your pieces to be assailed on any square. Players have
to move their pieces somewhere, somewhere is defined
by sixty-four squares, and the best somewhere is usually the center.

Unschooled players tend to choose squares near or

on the rim. There, they assume, their pieces will avoid endangered species status. And they are right, in a way. A piece placed on the outskirts can indeed be attacked from fewer squares than one situated in the center, and as such is safer from assault.

But to play the game successfully means learning to think in terms of attack and control, not just protection and defense. While we typically think about our own safety first, we won't make a mark in chess simply by guarding our forces. Players must think counter-intuitively. If they can be attacked less easily *on* the rim, they can also strike less easily *from* the rim. Besides, when restricted to the edge, there's no place to run.

The knight sitting on an outside row has the ability to reach no more than four squares. Consigned to the corner, the gallant crusader sits on the apex of despair, with little hope of relief. But put that piece in the center, and the knight becomes a powerful interloper, conceivably striking at as many as eight different squares.

Turn to the bishop. It generally observes more territory when positioned nearer the center, at the intersection of two long diagonals. Even the queen has greater mobility from the middle. Aside from the rook, which on an otherwise empty board covers the same area no matter where it's stationed, every chess unit finds its authority curtailed by sitting on the periphery.

Limit your forces and you limit your chances. That's why chess teachers routinely remind their students that knights placed on the rim are grim (or even dim). Eventually, good learners learn the lesson at hand: The center is better because it affords more opportunities.

But to come to that deduction, players have to hurdle over their initial assumptions. To win, you have to deliver checkmate. That usually requires heading into the thick of things, despite its attendant hazards. The natural prerequisite to taking reasonable risks is to play for control of the center.

No business can be run effectively if its players spend their energies merely protecting what they have. Business, like chess, is a competition. To compete means to advance—mindful of the risk, aware that if you don't take chances when the situation calls for it, you may perish. So stop the muddle. Take the middle.

- **Move away from the middle, but stay in the center.**

8.

Develop the Pieces

Chess point: To get the most out of your forces,
you must ready them from the start.

Picture this. A chessplayer starts attacking his opponent from the get-go. Playing White, he brings out his queen almost at once. He slides it from square to square, issuing one apparent threat after another to his adversary's king in the process.

His opponent deftly rebuffs every empty threat. He answers each queenly attack by developing his own troops further, and at the attacker's expense. Black deploys a knight, then a handy pawn, a rook, his own queen, and a bishop. Meanwhile, White winds up defending and retreating the only piece he has out, his lonely queen. After traveling to seven different locations, the white queen returns to take up residence on its original square, situated as if it hadn't moved at all. Who says you can never go home again?

The scenario is historical. The game, held in Mobile, Alabama, in the middle of the nineteenth century, pitted Louisianan master Paul Morphy (1837–1884) as Black against aficionado Judge A. B. Meek (1814–1865). The magistrate's wildly premature attack allowed Morphy to build an insurmountable lead in development. It took just twenty-one moves for the fellow from New Orleans to conquer.

Morphy was the first player to understand and practice the principle of development. He may have been the greatest player of all time, considering how far ahead he was of his contemporaries. Development wasn't a major nineteenth-century chess preoccupation. It became the businesslike way to play only when Morphy made it so.

Nowadays, players know better than to rely on a single piece to do their dirty work. It takes one nasty loss to find out that an attack without foundation has all the staying power of a New Year's resolution. Alert players use their opening moves to prospect for opportunities. They do this by consciously trying to get out a different piece on each turn instead of moving the same piece a number of times.

The two-headed chess monster, praxis and theory, has settled on a preferred sequence for development. We should start by setting our middle pawns in motion. Next, we try to develop our minor pieces (bishops and knights) and then our major ones (queen and rooks). The lighter forces lay the groundwork for subsequent invasion. Then the heavy artillery rumbles in, usually after we've safely tucked the king away by castling.

It was Morphy who taught chess people that early development is paramount to unbeatable technique. Morphy deduced that if he could develop his pieces efficiently, he'd gain time, the single most important advantage in the opening stages of a chess fight. Time is money in the business world. It can make or break you in the chess world.

It's really hard to play if our pieces never stir from their initial squares. So we aim to animate them immediately, issuing pesky threats in the bargain. As Napoléon said: "The essence of strategy is to have more force at the crucial point than the enemy." He should have known.

Development doesn't mean moving pieces anywhere under the tent, to any square that offers a legal choice. To mobilize adroitly, players have to find just the right place for a given piece. Then, like knowing generals, get it there with dispatch. Bring a unit out before you know where it belongs, and you may wind up losing time trying to get it to where it belonged in the first place. Time you've lost is time gained for your opponent. In the finest of all proactive worlds, your forces should advance to their desired squares as quickly as possible.

Nevertheless, beginning players intuitively assume that their king will be safe from attack only if strong sentries are hanging around to help defend the crown. They tend to enlist pawns right away, often letting their more capable fighters sleep in at home. But this strategy rarely works. An entire city can be toppled if its ranking officers are caught napping. It's called the Trojan War, and it happens every day on chessboards all over the planet.

Instead, players have to actuate all their pieces harmoniously. They must bolster each other's strengths to mete out attacks. Thus, they avoid putting a rook on a closed file. That would only limit its reach. Nor do they willingly block their bishop with a friendly pawn. That would deny it diagonal hope.

Pieces need purpose. Movement for movement's sake isn't good enough. Nor can players afford to push the same piece around several times without consequence. You can't play a team sport with only one player on the field, assuming the team, the sport, and the field are on the real side of the neutral zone.

Paul Morphy did more than just marshal his army. He showed that the best development was aggressive, simultaneously hard-hitting and dissuasive. You can play for the center, develop your pieces, and castle early. But if you can do all that while preventing your opponent from doing the same, you truly are the force behind the force.

The business arena has much in common with

chess. No company can conduct the sort of game Judge Meek played against Morphy, all untamed and ferocious attack with no substance. We've seen what happened when some dot-com companies were fashioned with little more than a catchy idea and some slick marketing. The business equivalent of a queen without footing got pushed around for a few moves. It may have been fun to watch a lot of quick and thrilling action, but it didn't lead to long-term achievement.

When can a business be deemed successful? When it's built on bedrock. This takes developing its resources, positioning each component of the firm in its best and most natural setting, and ensuring that all parts boast clear relationships with every other. The CEO who takes a page from Morphy's book does all this while restricting the competition's ability to do likewise.

There's a point here. If you don't develop your game and deter your opponent's now, there may not be a game later—not with you in it.

- **The meek shall inherit the first rank, if that.**

9.

Don't Overextend

Chess point: Promising moves can fail if
played too soon or without support.

The first world champion, Wilhelm Steinitz (1836–1900), pioneered counterintuitive chess. Paradox could be the way to success. The king was not purely to be protected. It could be strong, even aggressive. Pieces did not always have to be in the center. They could exert great power from the edge. What failed here might work there.

Against all apparent chess reason, Steinitz could actually win games by retreating. Like many of today's war-room strategists, the master deliberately hoped to lure his opponents into premature attacks. He'd move back. They'd advance. Then Steinitz would spring forward, taking advantage of his opponent's overstretched deployments. His student, William Napier, called it "trigger chess." "Advancing backward," was Harry's choice of words.

Great pioneers win advocates. A long and venerable line of devotees followed up on Steinitz's ideas, beginning with Aron Nimzovich (1886–1935). Nimzovich earned worldwide recognition for, among other things, writing the mother of all chess books, *My System*. Like Steinitz, he explored every aspect of the game. Like Steinitz, he found unexpected realities that changed chess forever.

Before Nimzovich, Black traditionally played to get an equal share of the center. White moved a central pawn. Black did the same. But as Steinitz had preached, Nimzovich practiced. He invented opening moves to trick his opponent into thinking he'd surrendered the center when he hadn't. His *hypermodern* beginnings for Black were designed to tempt White into overextending. He developed ways to capitalize if they did.

Moving forces into enemy territory without support is hazardous in any battle zone. You can reach too far even with the diminutive pawn. Move pawns too freely, too soon, or too close to your opponent, and they become susceptible to attack. Such pawns may be lost, or sobering concessions might have to be made to keep them.

Nimzovich's version of one well-known opening, the Sicilian Defense, aimed to entice White into premature and unsupported incursions of just this sort. Typically, as in most regular Sicilians, Black tries to control the territory in front of White's king-pawn before attacking it, so that the king-pawn can't move to safety if threatened. Theorists (and players) still assume it's easier to attack and capture what can't run away. But on the second move of the Sicilian Defense, Nimzovich dispensed with preventive measures altogether. Instead, he used a knight to attack White's pawn immediately, even though that pawn could still advance aggressively on the knight. His hope was to inveigle White into overreaching almost at once, to push the pawn too soon. To

White, the apple looked appetizing. But Nimzovich thought the inside had worms.

Entranced by Nimzovich's ideas, one of chess history's greatest players, Alexander Alekhine (1892–1946), took them a step further—and a step back. Literally. Instead of waiting until Black's second move, Alekhine tried playing the knight's siren call on Black's first move. He gave us Alekhine's Defense, which relies on assailing White's king-pawn without any preparation, proffering, in the bargain, the seductive challenge "Come and get me."

Bring in the innovative Richard Réti (1889–1929), who had the courage to take yet another quantum jump in the counterintuitive. If Nimzovich's ideas are so good for Black, why aren't they at least as good for White? He tried to find the answer during what some observers have characterized as the greatest chess game ever played: Réti vs. Alekhine, at Baden-Baden in 1925.

Réti's first move involved a pawn on the flank, and it neatly allowed Alekhine, as Black, to occupy the center with his own pawn. Alekhine did. Then Réti got even cuter. He used Alekhine's idea to intimidate Alekhine.

He brought out his knight, instantly assailing the target pawn, hoping to lure Black into a policy of over-extension. Alekhine seized the bait and forged ahead, advancing his pawn on White's knight. A great intellectual battle had been joined. Alekhine continued his offensive while Réti challenged Black's possibly over-extended forces.

The critical moment came at move twenty. Réti stood a little better, although perfect play on both sides probably would have led to a draw. Alekhine decided to play for one directly, bringing about the same position three times, in order to claim a draw by the threefold-repetition rule.

But Réti bit the bullet. Instead of accepting the draw, he aimed for more, without sufficient justification. He purposely played an inferior move to avoid repeating the position for a third time. To play for a win may have been a noble effort, but not a wise one, since it meant overextending his legions in the process. What he had planned to do to Alekhine would soon be done to him.

At the very end, after each player had tried to bait the other into going too far, one succeeded. Alekhine's bishop delivered a dramatically winning fork, exploiting the knight Réti had left out of position, vulnerable and overextended on the flank. Alekhine hadn't refuted counterintuitive play, just proven he could do it better.

Companies that don't watch over their resources—intellectual or material—can't secure their investment. Overextend your supply lines, and you can lose your business, just as you'd conclusively lose your chess game. If you neglect to make sure all the parts are harmoniously connected, the whole may fall apart. "There are two times in a man's life when he should not speculate," wrote Mark Twain. "When he can't afford it and when he can."

- **If you know you've gone too far, it's too late.**

10.

Convert Weaknesses into Strengths

Chess point: Practically every situation has hidden value for the opportunist.

Twenty-one-year-old Boris Spassky (b. 1937) sat down, just behind two rows of gleaming white chess pieces. Mikhail Tal, only a year older than his opponent, took his place as Black. It was 1958, and the Twenty-fifth USSR Chess Championship was well under way.

Both players were acutely aware of the stakes. The winner would take a significant step forward in the world championship cycle. The loser would be eliminated from the competition.

Two dozen moves into the game the players reached a roughly even position. Tal offered his opponent a draw. But Spassky declined, confident that he could take the game and reach the next rung on the ladder leading to the world championship crown. It seemed he was right. Three moves later, Tal made a slight mistake. Spassky had an edge, and he pressed hard to exploit it. He forced Tal's king out in the open, where he planned to attack it simultaneously with his queen and rook.

Under heavy pressure, Tal was forced to move his exposed king up the board. It appeared that Black was fighting a losing battle. A king left unsheltered and vulnerable in the opening and middle stages of a game is subject to menacing attacks from a bevy of unfriendly pieces. That's why players usually try to get their king castled early.

Clearly, Tal's exposed king seemed unsafe. But Spassky couldn't quite capitalize. Worse yet, his opponent was about to spin chess reality on its head. Instead of safeguarding his king, Tal did the opposite. He used it to spearhead an invasion! In just a few moves Tal's king went from victim to assailant, and Spassky was forced to resign.

Chess can be paradoxical. A weakness can become an asset in the hands and mind of a tenacious player. Any disadvantage on the board can disguise a possible advantage. A busted pawn structure laying the king open to attack? Imagine moving the king to the side, off the exposed file, so a rook can take its place. Suddenly set free, the rook can use the opened position for a laser attack. Your opponent may have hoped to use the file to get you. Now your rook can use it to get him.

Take a weak pawn. It often fails to fulfill its defensive mission. Left alone and helpless, it can also drain resources brought in to guard it. Forces are then tied down to its defense.

But there may be a better way. Instead of wasting time and resources protecting the pawn, combatants can change perspective, hoping to give the pawn away with advantage. Perhaps the opponent will have to compromise his own position to capture it. If he does, the pawn and its problems disappear with the defender's newly acquired counterattack.

In chess, a weakness will remain a liability if the

player doesn't find its hidden strength. Reversing one chess principle to unveil another, Tal demonstrated that a weak king could become a strong one, just like that.

Back in the midst of the Great Depression, a smart businessman acted with equally creative inspiration, and succeeded brilliantly because of it. In 1938, William Benton bought the Muzak Corporation. He did this knowing that serious musicians held Muzak in contempt.

Benton had chutzpah. So he made Muzak's lack of artistic merit his selling point. The new owner promptly invented a new slogan for the company: "Music not to be listened to." It became just what the doctor ordered—for his office. Barbershops, grocery stores, elevators, you hum it. Twenty years after that, Benton sold the company for a huge profit.

Over the sixty-four squares, weaker or less good can often be made stronger, better, or faster. The same diagonal principle holds for the business world. Turning a weakness into a strength is an attitude of mind. It means appreciating what you have, instead of despairing over what you don't.

Sometimes it takes special perception to imagine the flip side. But winning is not just about supposing. It's also about doing. And once you know how to make this into that, you can win at either side's game, from either side.

- **Some moves are right only because they're a little wrong.**

11.

Learn from Your Mistakes

Chess point: We progress by admitting our
blunders and understanding our losses.

Eight years without losing a game. A decade that
saw only a single loss. Earning and holding the
title of world champion for six years straight. As if acquiring all these honors were not enough, Cuban master
José Raúl Capablanca (1888–1942) once came in third
on *Esquire* magazine's list of the most attractive men in
the world. Back in 1927, only Rudolf Valentino and
Ramon Novarro could claim to be better-looking.

At times it seemed that Capablanca played perfect
chess. But accurate performers can blunder. Competing
in an international tournament in the 1930s, the Cuban

faltered for a second, allowing his opponent to gain a rook for a knight. It was a losing transaction, and Capablanca was down the equivalent of two pawns. Generally, when a player is that far behind in a major tournament, the contest is lost. Even so, the great master somehow managed to draw the game.

Capablanca was a proud man. Unable to bear the thought that anyone might think he'd made a mistake, he went out of his way to prove that he hadn't. A few rounds later, Capablanca was faced with the exact position in which he'd lost a rook for a knight just a few games before. With counterintuitive chic, he wittingly blundered in exactly the same way. Once again, he "lost" a rook for a knight, aiming to make his earlier error seem a deliberate choice. As critics drew their own conclusions, Capablanca drew another game.

Chess is a demanding discipline. It can take pounds off a competitor during a single game. Okay, not a thin one. But top-notch chess doesn't allow for fooling around. Capablanca purposely made a bad move in order to display his superior skill. He got away with chess murder.

Nevertheless, it's awkward to consider draws against inferior opponents as great triumphs. And though he could let pride get the better of him, Capablanca inherently understood how much more useful it is to learn from bad judgments than to deny one has made them. More than a decade before, the year he won the world championship, he published his seminal book *Chess Fundamentals*.

Surprisingly, the young champion decided to include a number of his losses in the work. He confessed that he had learned more from some of his defeats, as painful as they were, than he had from his most outstanding victories.

The prolific grandmaster and writer Savielly Tartakover once quipped: "The winner is usually the one who makes the next-to-last mistake." A lapse can endanger any given encounter. But it won't tally as a serious error until it's ignored or rationalized. That's how you lose games. And that's when you can expect that your past blunder will lead to future losses. Operate on the assumption that you don't (or can't) make mistakes and you learn nothing at all.

One day, I was hanging around in a corner of Washington Square Park, watching the filming of a motion picture. The crew wrapped, and I took off to visit my old haunt around the stone chess tables, where I had played so many offhand games as a teenager. I noticed a fellow intently studying a chess position at one of the far-off corner boards. Feeling a little nostalgic, I walked over and challenged him to a game. He accepted.

We hadn't been playing too long when I found a combination that led to a forced mate. I played it. Realizing that he was about to lose, my opponent wound up resigning. "What an original idea!" he declared. It wasn't, actually, and I knew it. But it took me a moment or two to remember why the final sequence and the circumstances seemed so familiar. Then it hit me. I had used exactly that motif some twenty years earlier, also in Washington Square Park, and at that very table.

Strangely, there was more to it. I looked up again at my opponent's face. It was, as Yogi Berra once said, déjà vu all over again. Some twenty years before I had played the same position in the same place against the same person! Who says you can't lose—or win—the same game twice?

My opponent's compliment aside, my moves hadn't been all that original—not even on the first try. During our first game (and our second), I'd used a trap learned from Russian research published in the early sixties, which I had consulted after losing a similar but different game myself. Then I'd gone searching for the right moves to a game I'd played entirely wrong. Motivated by a memorable defeat, I learned how to save myself. Twice.

Ignore a mistake and you'll make it again. Pretend that it was no mistake in the first place and you might get away with it, just as Capablanca did in the 1930s. But he didn't win that way, and neither will you. As Tartakover also said, "The blunders are all there, waiting to be made."

Mistakes are easily made. How? By forgoing an immediate attack in favor of needless vacillation. By attacking without preparation. By refusing to learn what you did wrong in the first (or second) place.

Players record their games and study past ones for various reasons. Certainly, they want to know where they went awry. They also want to fathom how they could have done better. If they've let their advantage slip away, they review their moves to see how they could have won for sure. If they've missed a saving opportunity, they try to figure out where they could have rescued themselves. They come to accept the good buy of losing now for discovering how to win later.

The business world is no less fluid a place than the chessboard, and each day the play changes. Businesspeople, too, record and analyze results. They study the past so they can profit in the future—the only future worth knowing. And if they're effective, they learn from their mistakes, especially not to repeat them.

- **The worst mistakes are those you think you haven't made.**

12.

Don't Sacrifice Without Good Reason

Chess point: Sacrifices should be made only if
they promise a clear advantage.

Once upon another chess time, in a chess world far, far away, the consummate German champion Emanuel Lasker (1868–1941) sat down to play against another great gamer, Geza Maroczy (1870–1951) of Hungary. The two grandmasters played in grandly aristocratic style, on a gentleman's wager. A large audience gathered to watch the long-anticipated game. Some placed bets on who would finish last.

In chess, as in life, most things have a price. The story goes that Lasker suggested playing with a special chess set. Each figure was represented by a drinking vessel of some sort or other. All, without exception, contained an alcoholic beverage. Each pawn was a little liqueur. Bishops and knights were glasses of wine. Every rook was a whiskey. And the queen, the most powerful piece on any board, became the most potent drink on this one, an entire bottle of bubbly. According to the rules of this spirited encounter, if you captured a piece, you had to drink its contents—right then.

The wily Lasker decided to play for the Scholar's Mate, where the queen is thrust into the game prematurely. It's an old trick that often works against inexperienced players, who haven't learned to look at their opponent's moves. Resorting to an ancient chess con against a grandmaster must have seemed downright ludicrous. Lasker's queen couldn't safely capture the pawn next to the Hungarian's king. Enter chess's theater of the absurd. Her Majesty took the pawn anyway, giving check in the bargain.

Casually, Lasker leaned back and downed the little pawn he had just captured. Maroczy, in a page out of Brecht, had no choice but to take the champ's queen to get out of check. This meant, however, that he had to quaff the champagne. Immediately. Maroczy found himself unable to continue, and Lasker won by default. No one knows who drank what afterward.

Lasker deliberately placed his queen where he had to lose it. Some onlookers may have concluded that the game's foremost authority had sacrificed his best piece. But Lasker foresaw that he'd succeed. That's important. What kind of sacrifice is it if you know you're going to win by doing it? Clearly, that's no sacrifice at all—not if we use language to think.

Pieces may be given up for a number of reasons, and doing so doesn't always constitute a true sacrifice. Ceding a queen for a rook (9 points for 5) is not a sacrifice if you haven't a choice. If you're just cutting losses, it's a salvage mission. If you lose something you didn't notice was threatened, that's a plain and simple blunder. And if you've exchanged one piece for another of equal value, that's a trade, not a sacrifice.

So if relinquishing a piece isn't necessarily a sacrifice, what is? In chess, a sacrifice is a willing offer of material in the service of a plan without an absolutely predictable outcome. The player makes a rational decision, entailing a calculated gamble. That explains why real sacrifices typically involve lesser units or subtleties in position, rather than valuable pieces like the queen. Jeopardizing even the smallest concerns in the face of uncertainty takes nerve.

Chess games are often won and lost by the tiniest of missteps, so no one can afford to speculate without concrete hope of gain. Generally, you shouldn't "sac," as chessplayer slang puts it, unless it's called for. You should only do so when it seems right.

Players must think on various levels during a game. They try to pair off temporary elements, like time and space, or lasting ones, like pawn structure and material. At any moment the transitional can outweigh the permanent. You can give up a piece to seize a square that grants total command of the board. Or you can jettison force in the short run to get it back on the other side of the equation, as Einstein pointed out so relatively.

But any sacrifice you make should be based on a plan that you sense is good, whether you have the proof in hand or not. Successful businesses operate in much the same way. There are always potential risks when you take the most measured stride. A company floods the market with a free product. It expects consumers to buy the commercial version. Will it work? Ultimately, you find out only if you try.

But you shouldn't even try unless logic and experience suggest that the chance you're taking is small, and you're likely to gain in the end. The rule for sacrifices in chess or life is simple. Sacrifice only if it looks like a good idea—after you've taken a peek at your future.

- **The smart ones sacrifice their opponent's pieces.**

13.

Seek Small Advantages

Chess point: Every chance to gain the smallest
superiority should be considered.

One day a famous European grandmaster walked
into the Marshall Chess Club to shoot the breeze.
The club occasionally suffered from a surfeit of players
spewing a little professional hot air, but this particular
gentleman's reflections were always masterful. I sat
down to listen in.

The venerable fellow began reminiscing. He told us
about the time he saw two world champions, Tigran
Petrosian (1929–1984) and Valery Smyslov (b. 1921),
play a peerless game. The two Russians had similar
styles. Both were careful and deliberate, shunning

showy attacks for building up small but certain advantages.

"I don't like this kind of chess. They play little moves," the European chess connoisseur announced in richly accented English. "Petrosian goes here," he lamented, moving a white pawn ahead half a square, "and Smyslov goes there." He reached out and moved a black pawn a quarter of a square. Neither move was legal. Players have to move figures from one square to another and not halfway or partially in between. But the maestro was busy making a point. He went on with his demonstration, announcing sadly, "Then Petrosian goes here." He took hold of the white pawn again and moved it almost imperceptibly forward. "They play little moves," the dejected grandmaster concluded. "This is not chess. I don't like this."

The truth is that big moves, ones that pose blatantly direct threats, don't usually lead to checkmate. They're too easy to spot and correspondingly easier to parry. Most experienced players, including the most mournful European chess aesthetes, play for small advantages, using the sort of "little moves" the grandmaster had grumbled about. They hunt and peck, hoping that any benefit they accrue will pan out. Opponents might dismiss a little nugget as trivial. Or overlook it altogether.

When newcomers arrive on the chess scene, they persist in looking for an apparently big moment, when they can capture a piece or deliver a check. It's an exciting feeling to take the opponent's knight or rook, and there's no doubt that openly attacking your opponent's king is a chessic delight. But these are often momentary triumphs that give an illusion of strength without yielding any real power. Giving check just to give check, without greater purpose, is often a waste of time. Capturing just to capture may be discarding your only chance to do something quieter but better.

Despite that reality, some of today's masters continue to favor sheer attack. And two centuries ago, almost everyone who inhabited the chess world praised grandiose and flashy tactics, independent of their accuracy or merit. Dramatic play backfires, however, when it relies on errors made by less competent players or when it recklessly exposes one's own position to a crushing counterattack.

Enter Wilhelm Steinitz (1836–1900), one of chess history's greatest theoreticians. Steinitz split from popular preferences for chess-playing flamboyance. The one-time Talmudic scholar pointed out that while playing for small advantages may be the more subtle and challenging strategy, it certainly constitutes the more reliable one.

What were those small advantages that Steinitz urged players to find and exploit? Nothing obvious, like impounding a loose piece or initiating a surprise mating attack. Steinitz's advantages were far more understated. They could include controlling a key square, or acquiring more room to operate. They could mean having a knight when a knight is better than a bishop, or a bishop when a bishop is superior to a knight. Steinitz's strategy included any number of other factors that might seem slight and indefinable, even to veteran players.

Accumulate advantages, Steinitz claimed, and they will snowball. Eventually, the only way your opponent can stop such a patient accrual is by surrendering material, no matter how little. After a few such minor concessions are made, and the situation settles down, the position may not look radically different. But one important thing is likely to have changed. By remaining true to Steinitz's theory of positional chess, the superior side will probably have gained something palpable.

Indeed, Steinitz posed players a heavy-duty intellectual test. To think through each aspect of any given chess position, to consider and chart the effect of the smallest movement on the board, to appraise and reassess at every point, requires dogged discipline. When both sides are so tuned, it can lead to great symphonies of chess play, where every nuance meets its counterpoint in comparably orchestrated subtlety. No one loses and chess art wins.

A nearly undetectable gain may turn out to be decisive. Steinitz was the first player to understand that little moves can be significant, that long-term, well-nurtured thinking is required to reach the goal. This is scarcely a mere chess truth. Lao-tzu's oft-quoted "A journey of a thousand miles begins with a single step" is used by practically anyone teaching anything and by many teaching nothing.

We laud entrepreneurial spirit in this country just as we admire original play on a chessboard. But those who enter the business world as self-styled mavericks will seldom become permanent residents there on the basis of a few ostentatious moves. It doesn't matter if it seems colorful. It matters if it works. The business that takes planned, careful, and incremental steps is far more likely to achieve enduring goals. We'll still be depending on that company long after many yet-to-be ones are gone.

Peter Lynch, who was named one of the greatest investors of all time by *The Wall Street Journal*, once wrote a "Final Checklist" for would-be investors. "Long shots," he pointed out dryly, "almost never pay off." And Michael Dell, CEO of Dell computers, once compared business to baseball à la Steinitz. "Swing for hits," he wrote, "not home runs. Go for the highest batting average rather than trying to hit a home run every time." The result is a steady gain, one you can count on when the scores are totted up.

If you want success, value dedication over dazzle, the sure thing over pie in the sky. It's big chess and good business to think big and good in small ways.

• You can go far without going far away.

14.

Don't Apply Principles Mechanically

Chess point: Specific moves always prevail
over general rules.

The U.S. Chess Championship. The Henry Hudson Hotel, New York City. The best players in America. Round number three. Bobby Fischer (b. 1943) was set to play one of his most memorable games ever, against *New York Times* chess columnist Robert Byrne.

I was there for the duration of the tournament. From December 1963 to January 1964 I worked as a wall boy, moving pieces on large demonstration boards so the audience could follow the games. Fortune had grinned widely at me. On that day, I stood close enough to the Fischer-Byrne contest to be able to check out some breathtaking action.

On the twelfth move, Fischer advanced in the center, inviting a trade. Players trade like for like, or comparable for comparable. A desirable trade usually delivers an advantage, whether obvious or implied. Players trade to solve problems. But they also do so to gain time, space, mobility, king safety, or other positional improvements.

To some, Fischer's trade seemed a little blunderous. He had poised his forces for attack, but simultaneously incurred a seriously weak pawn—a potential target for White's forces. On the fifteenth move, Fischer took another step into the Valley of Death. He gave up a knight for a pawn. Once again he'd opted for attack. This time at the cost of material. It seemed that Fischer had violated a basic chess tenet, sacrificing without good reason.

Apparently, Fischer was prepared to defy chess principle once more. Just three moves later, when he had the chance to even up the piece-and-pawn count by taking Byrne's rook, Fischer unaccountably reached for his opponent's bishop instead. Was this brilliantly counterintuitive or egregiously bad?

Startled expressions across the room suggested the latter. A rook, after all, is worth two pawns more than a bishop, and Fischer needed to take the rook—not the bishop—in order to regain the property he'd lost surrendering a knight for a pawn. Most of us wondered what transgression of principle would come next.

After a flurry of moves, Fischer remained significantly behind in material, down by about two pawns in value. He pushed his queen up one space so that it could invade on a square formerly defended by the bishop he'd destroyed. Whatever his plan, it didn't look to provide enough compensation for his material deficit. Few doubted it. Fischer was in trouble.

Afterward, I learned about the discussion taking place in a nearby room, where masters and master kibitzers could dissect games without interfering with the players. Two grandmasters had determined that Fischer was dead lost. His game was doomed because he'd thrown away both material *and* position. They concluded that Fischer would resign, possibly after Byrne's next move.

Just then they got word from the floor. Fischer couldn't resign. Byrne already had.

Byrne had analyzed the position and saw the chess writing on the board. He was about to go down, and there was no recourse. Fischer had launched a crushing invasion that his opponent hadn't predicted and couldn't stop. It was mystifying, Byrne admitted later. With all his pieces so well developed, White was helpless against Black's onslaught.

Fischer's win was printed worldwide with the highest chess praise, an exclamation point! The enfant terrible from Brooklyn, my hometown, dominated the last eight games. It was the only time, before or since, that any player won the U.S. Chess Championship by a shutout.

Why hadn't keen observers perceived Fischer's plan? Because they were hooked on basic principles, and stopped thinking as soon as they'd employed them.

According to general chess theory, you shouldn't cede substance unless you can find a way to recoup it, which usually means getting back equal value or better. Every transaction is made in order to return some small advantage that can become noteworthy later.

In this instance, however, Fischer achieved the end goal far differently than the grandmasters envisioned. He wasn't after the very least the application of principle could offer, but the most. He applied principles mindfully and appropriately, as they really pertained. And like a gladiator, Fischer played for his life.

To win at chess you have to do more than gain time, improve your position, or annex more material. You have to integrate it all to deliver checkmate. Reciting platitudes won't do it. You have to get specific to the situation and concrete in your analysis. You don't play principles. You play moves. *They* decide your fate; clichés don't.

Keep your eyes on the goal. Fischer knew the concessions he was making would grant him far more than a small positional edge. They would prevent Byrne from defending his king. Fischer thought diagonally, cutting through the stumbling blocks. He reduced the complexity of the game to its essence: checkmate.

General assumptions are often necessary, but they can't be allowed to thwart the analytic process. Principles can guide us to the goal line, but they can't score the points. Fischer understood that giving up material in exchange for total positional dominance was cardinal. Perhaps this was too subtle for most of the audience. Fischer saw further, but then, he was actually looking.

Holiday Inn creator Kemmons Wilson once defined the expedient mind: "Opportunity," Wilson wrote, "knocks as often as you have an ear trained to hear it, an eye trained to see it, a hand trained to grasp it, and a head trained to use it."

To spot unique opportunity, you must discover before you analyze. That means thinking flexibly and interpreting rules creatively—their rules or yours. What seems small may be serious and significant. What looks complicated may have a simple solution. However you do your accounting, you can't afford to apply principles mechanically. If you do, you're supposing instead of thinking, and that won't win very much at all.

- **A principle tells you where to look, not what to see.**

15.

Strive for More than You Need

Chess point: By playing at full throttle you get
more from your efforts and avoid letdowns.

In those days, Los Angeles was famous for its terrible
air, not its chess. Nevertheless, during the summer
dog days of 1963, the world's greatest players gathered
on the West Coast for the First Piatigorsky Cup, an
international grandmasters' chess tournament.

During the fourth round, former USSR champion
Paul Keres (1916–1975) faced the Icelandic grandmaster Fridrik Olafsson (b. 1935), who was at that point
undefeated. Some forty moves into the challenge, Olafsson appeared to be winning yet another game. When
the contest was adjourned, his tasks seemed uncompli-

cated: to rest, analyze some key lines, and return the next day to tend his advantage.

But chess demands that its proponents expect the unexpected. Olafsson came back on cruise control when Keres hadn't quite dispatched his torpedoes. The Russian, long known for his tenacious counterpunching, placed one obstacle after another in his opponent's way. He was so determined, so persistent, and so chessically obnoxious that he ended up throwing Olafsson completely off. The befuddled Icelander missed an immediate win. Worse, he lost his equilibrium. Down he went, after a titanic endgame struggle. Buoyed by this reversal of fortune, Keres sailed on to prevail in several other critical games, sharing the top prize with then world champion Tigran Petrosian (1929–1984).

Players on the verge of victory must never assume that the contest will play itself out. As German master Siegbert Tarrasch (1862–1934) so cogently stated, "The hardest thing is to win a won game." To convert an advantage into achievement, real competitors aim for the most precise technique they can find. They expect heroic defiance and wage ongoing war to ensure that ultimate control is never relinquished. Strong players always play for more than they need in order to get what they really want.

And champions don't simply surrender when they're losing, not as long as they feel they have any chances left. When they're behind, they pull out every stop. They understand that any opportunity, any possibility, any perceived gain can be used to twist the other player's assumed conquest into one of their own. Keres won because he refused to lose.

Yet what if trying for more is purely foolhardy or downright impossible? There are times when you can't reasonably expect to win a game. All is not lost, though, because you can reset your mindset and focus on how not to lose. In chess this is called a draw, and it beats utter defeat any day, any time. In fact, by drawing, you may be able to maintain your overall advantage in the competition. Maybe you can stay ahead of the player who hoped to put you away. Sometimes a draw might do things a loss never could, from saving face to clinching a championship.

Such was exactly the case when world champion

Emanuel Lasker confronted José Raúl Capablanca during the seventh of ten final rounds in the famous St.
Petersburg tournament of 1914. Capablanca was ahead
by a point and a half, and it looked as though he needed
nothing more than a draw to take the entire competition.
The truth was, he could afford to drop the game to Lasker and still finish ahead in the tournament. Lasker, in
contrast, needed at least a win to have any chance at
capturing first prize.

Remarkably, it appeared as if Lasker was prepared to
make Capablanca's easy job easier. He promptly shocked
everyone by forcing a sudden queen exchange early in the
game, greatly simplifying the situation. Since Capablanca's position was sound, most observers assumed he
could get an easy draw merely by avoiding trouble. His
opponent's strategy seemed to make no sense.

But Lasker knew that Capablanca had expected a
complex middlegame. He had tried to disarm the Cuban
by giving him what he least expected, catapulting him
toward what seemed to be a cut-and-dry endgame. He
succeeded. Baffled by Lasker's unusual tactics, Capablanca dithered, played nervously, and lost. He faltered

again in the very next round. Lasker pulled ahead to cop the top prize.

Lasker, who needed a victory, played for one by deception. Capablanca, who needed only a draw, played too indecisively to earn even that. He was lulled into complacency over his standing in the tournament, and it cost him.

How does a player fight for a draw? By doing the same thing a good player does in trying to win. By committing fully, by extracting everything possible out of the position. The message is the same, no matter the game. To get what you want, play for more than you need—and it's not play.

That's advice for the business world. You can be winning, but that doesn't mean the battle has been won. When you're losing, you're going to go down unless you fight back. You can't just acquiesce. That simply doesn't work. To get the most, you have to give the most. You have to reach beyond, and then beyond that. And that's just the start.

- **You never get more than you settle for.**

Conclusion: Chess, a Final Frontier

The lesson is over. The pieces all sit on their assigned opening squares, awaiting some eventual contest. I get ready to leave, thinking about my student's upcoming tournament. So I remind him. Act as if the fate of humanity comes down to your play, I say. It really does.

Because of a chess game? How important can the outcome of someone else's leisure time be to the rest of us? Why should a knight's move change anything?

It doesn't. And it does. At the opposite end of one truth is another truth. When players grapple over a chessboard, they're not just playing chess. They're using one world to learn about another.

Playing chess nurtures what we need. We must have mental dexterity to survive. Analyzing, seeing ahead, calculating, reconsidering, strategizing, evaluating, sequencing, reasoning independently, thinking convergently—these are the chess moves that advance civilization.

To understand complex and interlocking relationships, you have to solve problems step by step. You have to think in layers, evaluating several factors simultaneously. And you'll need to use training and experience to develop an intuitive sense of how things work. However you seek an answer, use the most direct path. That's the diagonal way.

By delivering one challenge after another, by forcing us to think through a difficult puzzle without losing heart, by presenting us with unique patterns we may never see again, yet ought to pursue, chess becomes a partner in courage and imagination. It's not just a game, and we're not merely pawns in it. It's an entrepreneurial venture, and each one of us is J. P. Morgan.

You can tap that lesson anywhere, from board game to board meeting, from piece exchange to stock exchange. Your actions are based on your beliefs. Your beliefs form the foundation for your commitments. Be convinced of the value of what you do and you are certain to succeed. Once you accept that the fate of humanity depends on your efforts, it really does.

Chessary
How Chessplayers Use Language

Advantage Any kind of superiority.

Analysis An examination of moves and position.

Analyze To investigate in detail.

Attack A potential capture; to threaten.

Bishop The piece that moves only on diagonals.

Black The player who moves second at the start; initially, the defender; the darker-colored pieces.

Blunder A serious mistake; usually a move that changes the way the position is to be evaluated, throwing away a winning advantage or speeding up defeat.

Calculation The analysis of specific sequences of moves.

Capture A move; the removal of one unit by another; to take.

Castle To move the king and rook on the same turn.

Center The middle four squares and surrounding area.

Checkmate The end of the game, when the king would be captured on the next move.

Chess Clock A timing device with two clocks, one for each player.

Counterattack An attack mounted by the defender; to do so.

Counterintuitive Contrary to what you would expect, characterized by diagonal thinking.

Deductive Reasoning Calculating specific tactics and moves.

Defender The player or unit under attack; Black at the start.

Defense A protection or response to attack; Black's opening.

Develop To move a piece to a better place or improve its scope.

Development Preparing pieces for action.

Diagonal A slanted row of same-colored squares.

Diagonal Thinking Problem-solving using counter-intuitive shortcuts.

Draw A game where neither player wins or loses.

Elements Factors determining who has the advantage in a chess position; in the main: time, space, material, pawn structure, and king safety.

Endgame The third and final phase of a chess game.

Ending Another name for endgame.

Exchange An equal trade; also, difference in value between a rook and a minor piece.

Exchange Values The relative values of the pieces.

Exhibition A game or games played for the public.

File A vertical row of squares.

First Rank The horizontal row closest to the player.

Force The element of material; also, to control an opponent's moves.

Gambit A voluntary sacrifice in the opening.

Grandmaster The highest official rank a chessplayer can achieve.

Hypermodern Pertaining to a school or style developed in the early twentieth century advocating counterintuitive opening principles.

Illegal Move A move that can't be played.

Inductive Reasoning Developing strategies and plans; solving problems by generalization.

Initiative The ability to attack and control the play.

Intuition Problem-solving based on pattern recognition and experience.

Kibitzer An annoying bystander who talks too much.

King The piece both sides are trying to trap and capture.

Knight The piece that moves like a capital L.

Legal Move A move that can be played.

Line Any rank, file, or diagonal; also, a sequence of moves.

Lose To get checkmated, resign, forfeit on time, or be disqualified.

Lost Game A game that should lose even with best play by the defender.

Major Piece A queen or rook.

Maneuver To reposition a piece; the act of doing so.

Master An unofficial title for a strong player.

Match A set of games between the same players or teams.

Mate Short for checkmate.

Material An element; the pieces and pawns, collectively or individually.

Middlegame The second phase of a chess game; often characterized by strategy.

Minor Pieces Bishops and knights.

Mobility The freedom and ability to move pieces individually and as a group.

Move A turn for either side; the transfer of a unit from one square to another.

Opening The beginning phase of a chess game.

Open Line A rank, file, or diagonal unobstructed by pawns.

Patzer An experienced but weak player who thinks he's strong.

Pawn The weakest and most numerous unit; a symbol for helplessness.

Pawn-Grabbing Taking pawns riskily.

Pawn Structure An element; all aspects of pawn placement and dynamics.

Piece Either a king, queen, rook, bishop, or knight, but not a pawn.

Positional Concerned with small points and long-term effects.

Positional Advantage Any nonmaterial advantage.

Positional Chess A style of play that aims to accumulate small but safe advantages.

Principle A general truth, guideline, or piece of advice; not a rule.

Promotion The rule allowing a pawn to be changed into a new piece.

Queen The most powerful piece, able to move in any straight line.

Queening Promoting a pawn to a queen.

Rank A horizontal row of squares.

Resign To give up before being checkmated.

Rook The piece that moves horizontally or vertically.

Sac Short for sacrifice.

Sacrifice A voluntary surrender of material.

Simplify To avoid complications and trade pieces; a strategy usually employed when ahead in material or under attack.

Simultaneous Exhibition A public display where one player faces a number of players at different boards; also called a *simul*.

Space The element concerned with territory and mobility, determined by control and freedom of movement.

Stalemate A game drawn when the player to move is not checkmated but has no legal move.

Strategy General thinking; the opposite of tactics.

Tactics Specific threats; the opposite of strategy.

Take To capture a unit.

Tempo A move defined as a unit of time.

Threat A move that must be heeded.

Threaten To attack in a serious way; usually, aiming to capture with advantage.

Time The element concerned with the initiative, measured in moves.

Tournament A contest in which a number of players compete.

Trade An exchange of equal material; also, to make such a transaction.

Trap A tricky way to win; also, to snare.

Trapped Piece A piece that can't get to safety.

Unit Any piece or pawn.

Variation Any sequence of moves.

Visualization The ability to see possible moves in the mind.

Weakness Usually, a hard-to-guard pawn or square.

White The player who moves first at the start; initially, the attacker; the lighter-colored pieces.

Winning Having an advantage that should win.

Won Game A game that should be won with the best play.

Acknowledgments

I would like to thank the Thiede family for their participation in this project. Editorial consultant Dr. Barbara Thiede helped shape this book with visions and revisions. Her husband and son, Professor Ralf Thiede and Erik Thiede, read the manuscript in its various stages; their contributions were much appreciated. I would like to thank my agent, Richard Abate, for all his contributions and for putting up with my nonsense, and my editor, Peternelle van Arsdale, for her insight and for overseeing the enterprise from inception to completion.